GW01161941

2017

JANUARY

M	T	W	T	F	S	S
						1
2	3	4	5	6	7	8
9	10	11	12	13	14	15
16	17	18	19	20	21	22
23	24	25	26	27	28	29
30	31					

FEBRUARY

M	T	W	T	F	S	S
		1	2	3	4	5
6	7	8	9	10	11	12
13	14	15	16	17	18	19
20	21	22	23	24	25	26
27	28					

MARCH

M	T	W	T	F	S	S
		1	2	3	4	5
6	7	8	9	10	11	12
13	14	15	16	17	18	19
20	21	22	23	24	25	26
27	28	29	30	31		

APRIL

M	T	W	T	F	S	S
					1	2
3	4	5	6	7	8	9
10	11	12	13	14	15	16
17	18	19	20	21	22	23
24	25	26	27	28	29	30

MAY

M	T	W	T	F	S	S
1	2	3	4	5	6	7
8	9	10	11	12	13	14
15	16	17	18	19	20	21
22	23	24	25	26	27	28
29	30	31				

JUNE

M	T	W	T	F	S	S
			1	2	3	4
5	6	7	8	9	10	11
12	13	14	15	16	17	18
19	20	21	22	23	24	25
26	27	28	29	30		

JULY

M	T	W	T	F	S	S
					1	2
3	4	5	6	7	8	9
10	11	12	13	14	15	16
17	18	19	20	21	22	23
24	25	26	27	28	29	30
31						

AUGUST

M	T	W	T	F	S	S
	1	2	3	4	5	6
7	8	9	10	11	12	13
14	15	16	17	18	19	20
21	22	23	24	25	26	27
28	29	30	31			

SEPTEMBER

M	T	W	T	F	S	S
				1	2	3
4	5	6	7	8	9	10
11	12	13	14	15	16	17
18	19	20	21	22	23	24
25	26	27	28	29	30	

OCTOBER

M	T	W	T	F	S	S
						1
2	3	4	5	6	7	8
9	10	11	12	13	14	15
16	17	18	19	20	21	22
23	24	25	26	27	28	29
30	31					

NOVEMBER

M	T	W	T	F	S	S
		1	2	3	4	5
6	7	8	9	10	11	12
13	14	15	16	17	18	19
20	21	22	23	24	25	26
27	28	29	30			

DECEMBER

M	T	W	T	F	S	S
				1	2	3
4	5	6	7	8	9	10
11	12	13	14	15	16	17
18	19	20	21	22	23	24
25	26	27	28	29	30	31

NOTES

SPECIAL DATES

JANUARY
....
....
....

FEBRUARY
....
....
....

MARCH
....
....
....

APRIL
....
....
....

MAY
....
....
....

JUNE
....
....
....

JULY

AUGUST

SEPTEMBER

OCTOBER

NOVEMBER

DECEMBER

DEC 2016/JAN 2017

26 — MONDAY

27 — TUESDAY

28 — WEDNESDAY

29 — THURSDAY

30 — FRIDAY

31 — SATURDAY

1 — SUNDAY

RAISED GAME PIE

Raised pies have been a favourite of the British table for centuries, at one time majestic, elaborate constructions decorated with pastry columns, crests and coats of arms. This is a slightly more restrained version, but it is still a great-looking centrepiece for a party. A mixture of venison, rabbit, pheasant, pigeon or wild boar (according to what game you like, and what is available) is encased in crisp and rich, hot-water-crust pastry, which traps all the savoury meat juices without becoming soggy.

JANUARY

2   **MONDAY**

New Year's Holiday (UK & Republic of Ireland)

3 Back to School.   **TUESDAY**
Eva back

Holiday (Scotland)

4 Ethan back   **WEDNESDAY**

5 Ethan eye appt.   **THURSDAY**

6 Coffee with Paula   **FRIDAY**

7 Ethan - rugby - Ballymena.   **SATURDAY**

8 Take kids' Church .   **SUNDAY**

RAISED GAME PIE

SERVES 12

Kit you'll need:

1 large, oval raised/game pie mould OR a 20cm round spring-clip tin, 7cm deep, greased with lard; a 2.5cm oak leaf cutter OR leaf-shaped cutter; a baking sheet

For The Filling

700g boneless mixed game meat, diced
200g rindless back bacon, diced
200g minced pork belly (unsmoked)
2 banana shallots, finely chopped
2 garlic cloves, crushed
2 tablespoons Madeira
½ teaspoon ground mace
½ teaspoon ground allspice
2 tablespoons chopped fresh parsley
2 tablespoons chopped fresh thyme
salt and pepper, to taste

For The Hot-Water-Crust Pastry

450g plain flour
100g strong white bread flour
75g chilled unsalted butter, cut into 1cm cubes
200ml water
½ teaspoon salt
100g lard

To Glaze

1 egg yolk, beaten

JANUARY

9 — MONDAY

10 — TUESDAY

11 — WEDNESDAY

12 — THURSDAY

13 — FRIDAY

14 — SATURDAY

15 — SUNDAY

RAISED GAME PIE

1 Start by making the filling so the flavours have time to develop. Put all the ingredients into a large bowl. Add a little salt and pepper, then mix everything together with your hands until thoroughly combined. Take a teaspoon of the mixture, shape it into a small 'burger' and fry it for a minute or so on each side until cooked through, then taste and add more seasoning to the filling mixture, if necessary. Cover and chill while you make the pastry.

2 Heat the oven to 200°C/400°F gas 6. Combine both flours and a pinch of salt in a mixing bowl. Add the butter and rub in lightly using your fingertips. Pour the water into a small pan and add the salt and lard. Heat gently until the lard has melted, then bring to the boil. Pour the hot mixture on to the flour and quickly mix everything together with a wooden spoon to make a dough. As soon as the dough is cool enough to handle, tip it out on to a floured worktop and knead it just until smooth and even.

3 This pastry becomes crumbly as it cools, so you need to work quickly now. Cut off a third of the pastry and wrap it tightly in clingfilm. Roll out the remaining pastry to an oval or disc large enough to line your tin. Carefully lift the pastry into the tin and press it on to the base and side, smoothing out wrinkles. Leave excess pastry hanging over the rim. Check there are no cracks or holes in the pastry case – press the pastry together or patch with small scraps of pastry.

4 Roll out the remaining pastry to an oval or disc, slightly larger than the top of your tin, to form the lid. Cover with clingfilm and leave on the worktop for now.

5 Spoon the filling into the pastry-lined tin and press it down well, making sure the surface is level. Brush the edge of the pastry case with beaten egg yolk, then lay the pastry lid on top. Press the edges of the case and lid together firmly to seal. Trim off the excess pastry and crimp or flute the edge neatly. Make a hole in the centre of the lid to allow steam to escape during baking.

6 Gather up the pastry trimmings and roll them out again. Stamp out 20 leaves with the shaped cutter. Attach these to the pastry lid, using a dab of beaten egg yolk as glue. Brush the lid all over with beaten egg yolk to glaze.

7 Set the tin on the baking sheet and bake in the heated oven for 30 minutes. Turn down the oven temperature to 170°C/325°F/gas 3 and bake the pie for a further 1¾ hours until the pastry is a rich golden brown.

8 Leave the pie in its tin until completely cold before unmoulding. Serve at room temperature, on a rimmed plate to catch any juices. Store any leftovers, tightly wrapped, in the fridge.

JANUARY

16 — MONDAY

17 Open Night SW. — TUESDAY

18 — WEDNESDAY

19 — THURSDAY

20 — FRIDAY

21 — SATURDAY

22 — SUNDAY

NOTES

JANUARY

23 — MONDAY

24 — TUESDAY

25 — WEDNESDAY

26 — THURSDAY

27 — FRIDAY

28 — SATURDAY

Chinese New Year
29 — SUNDAY

NOTES

JANUARY / FEBRUARY

30   MONDAY

31   TUESDAY

1   WEDNESDAY

2   THURSDAY

3   FRIDAY

4   SATURDAY

5   SUNDAY

CHOCOLATE BROWNIES

Who can resist a brownie? This rich brownie is made from high-quality dark chocolate and uses a combination of the melted and whisked methods to create that signature squishy texture.

FEBRUARY

6 — MONDAY

7 — TUESDAY

8 — WEDNESDAY

9 — THURSDAY

10 — FRIDAY

11 — SATURDAY

12 — SUNDAY

NOTES

FEBRUARY / MARCH

27   MONDAY

(P)

28   TUESDAY

1   WEDNESDAY

Ash Wednesday & St. David's Day (Wales)

2   THURSDAY

3   FRIDAY

4   SATURDAY

5   SUNDAY

PRALINE & CHOCOLATE VOL-AU-VENTS

Literally 'flying with the wind', vol-au-vents are intended to be the lightest, wispiest of pastry mouthfuls, so this is a recipe to show off your pastry skills. The little cases are filled with dark ganache, hazelnut praline 'butter' and Crème Légère, the lightest of all Crème Pâtissières, to create layers of flavour. Beautifully presented, with curls of dark chocolate and flowers, these would make a sensational tiered display.

MARCH

6 — MONDAY

7 — TUESDAY

8 — WEDNESDAY

9 — THURSDAY

10 — FRIDAY

11 — SATURDAY

12 — SUNDAY

PRALINE & CHOCOLATE VOL-AU-VENTS

MAKES 24

Kit you'll need:
A 3cm and a 5cm plain round cutter; a baking sheet, lined with baking paper; a silicone sheet; 2 disposable piping bags.

For The Puff Pastry
300g plain flour
½ teaspoon salt
185ml icy cold water
250g unsalted butter
1½ tablespoons cocoa powder

For The Praline Butter
70g blanched hazelnuts
70g caster sugar
2 teaspoons water

For The Ganache
60g dark chocolate (50-60% cocoa solids), finely chopped
2 teaspoons espresso
60ml double cream (not extra-thick or 'spoonable')

For The Crème Légère
100ml full-fat milk
1 large egg yolk, at room temperature
1 tablespoon cornflour
20g caster sugar
10g unsalted butter, at room temperature
¼ teaspoon vanilla bean paste
75ml double cream (not extra thick or 'spoonable'), well chilled

To Finish
50g chopped toasted hazelnuts
50g dark chocolate (about 70% cocoa solids)
24 small purple pansies (optional)

MARCH

13 — MONDAY

14 — TUESDAY

15 — WEDNESDAY

16 — THURSDAY

17 — FRIDAY

St. Patrick's Day Holiday (Ireland)
18 — SATURDAY

19 — SUNDAY

PRALINE & CHOCOLATE VOL-AU-VENTS

1 To make the puff pastry, put the flour and salt into a bowl of a free-standing electric mixer fitted with the paddle attachment. Mix well, then add the cold water and, on low speed, work just until the ingredients come together to make a rough, shaggy dough. If there are dry crumbs add more water a tablespoon at a time. Turn out on to a lightly floured worktop and shape into a rectangle about 1cm thick. Wrap in clingfilm and chill for 15 minutes

2. Meanwhile, put butter between two sheets of clingfilm and pound with a rolling pin until supple but still very cold. Shape into a square with 12cm sides.

3. Roll out the dough away from you on the lightly floured worktop to a 13x25cm rectangle. Set the butter on the dough so it almost covers the bottom half of the rectangle. Fold over the dough to enclose the butter, then press the edges together to seal. Gently rollout the dough away from you to a 15x30cm rectangle. Mark the centre of a long side, then fold the bottom edge up to this centre point and fold the top down, so the short sides meet. Now fold the dough over in half to complete your first 'book turn'. Repeat, to give the dough another book turn, after rolling out the pastry for the second 'book fold', sift the cocoa over the rectangle before folding. Then cover with clingfilm and chill for 20 minutes. Repeat the process 2 more times so the dough has a total of 6 book turns. Wrap and chill for 30 minutes.

4. Shape the vol-au-vent cases, then bake at 200°C/400°F/gas 6 in the same way. Leave to cool while you make the fillings. Reduce the oven temperature to 180°C/350°F/gas 4.

5 To make the praline butter, put the hazelnuts in a small baking dish or tin and toast in the oven for 5-7 minutes until just starting to colour. Leave to cool. Line the baking sheet with clean baking paper or the silicone sheet. Put the sugar and water in a small pan, set over low heat and stir gently until the sugar has completely dissolved. Turn up the heat and boil, without stirring, until the syrup turns to a light caramel.

6 Add the hazelnuts and stir gently with a metal spoon, then cook for a few seconds longer until you have a rich caramel. Pour on to the lined baking sheet and leave to cool. Once completely cold and set, break into chunks, then put into a food processor and 'pulse' long enough to make a smooth, creamy 'butter'. Transfer to a bowl, cover and set aside until needed.

7 For the ganache, put the chopped chocolate and coffee into a heatproof bowl. Heat the cream until it just comes to the boil, then pour it over the chocolate. Leave to melt for a couple of minutes before stirring gently until smooth. Allow to cool and thicken up slightly, then transfer to a piping bag.

8 Press down the risen base in each pastry case, to make room for the filling. Snip off the tip of the piping bag to make a 5mm opening, then pipe a spiral of ganache into each pastry case. Leave to set at room temperature.

9 Meanwhile, make Crème Légère. Heat the milk in a small pan until almost boiling; remove from the heat. Beat the egg yolk with the cornflour and sugar in a heatproof bowl until smooth and light, then stir in the hot milk. When thoroughly combined, pour the mixture back into the pan and stir over medium/low heat until it boils and thickens. Remove from the heat and stir in the butter and vanilla. Transfer to a clean, heatproof bowl and press a piece of clingfilm on the surface to prevent a skin from forming, then leave to cool. Chill for 30 minutes.

10 Whip the cream until it will stand in soft peaks. Stir the chilled crème until it is very smooth, then fold it into the whipped cream. Transfer to the other piping bag and keep in the fridge if not using immediately.

11 To assemble the vol-au-vents, spoon a little praline butter on top of the set ganache in each pastry case. Snip off the end of the piping bag to make a 5mm opening and pipe a little crème légère on the praline butter. Sprinkle with a few chopped hazelnuts, then cover with a little more piped crème légère. Decorate one half of each filled vol-au-vent with a sprinkling of chopped hazelnuts.

12 Make shavings from the dark chocolate (see below) and use to decorate the top of the vol-au-vents. Arrange the pastries on a serving plate and decorate with some purple pansies, if you like. Serve immediately.

TIP: Chocolate curls & shavings
Gently melt 50g dark chocolate (about 70% cocoa solids), then pour it on to a clean marble slab or worktop. Working quickly, before the chocolate sets, use a palette knife to spread the chocolate thinly. Keep working the chocolate with the knife, spreading it back and forth, until you have a rough rectangle about 20 x 30cm and 2-3mm thick. As soon as the chocolate becomes matt and dull, rather than shiny, and starts to set, stop working it. Hold a large, sharp knife (pointing away from you), with the blade at an angle of about 45 degrees, on one side of the chocolate slab and scrape off a very thin sheet, which will curl as you go. For large curls, scrape from one side of the chocolate slab to the other. Take shorter shavings too. Use a palette knife, rather than your fingers, to gently lift the curls or shavings into place.

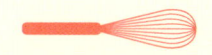

MARCH

20   MONDAY

21   TUESDAY

22   WEDNESDAY

23   THURSDAY

24   FRIDAY

25   SATURDAY

26   SUNDAY

Mothering Sunday (UK) & Daylight Saving Begins

NOTES

MARCH / APRIL

27 — MONDAY

28 — TUESDAY

29 — WEDNESDAY

30 — THURSDAY

31 — FRIDAY

1 — SATURDAY

2 — SUNDAY

FLORENTINE PASTRIES

Traditional Florentine biscuits, combining sticky nuts and candied fruits, are lacily thin and fragile. In this more substantial version, the mixture is held together on a crisp, rich pâte sucrée base – made in the classic way, straight on the worktop, not in a bowl, using egg yolks rather than water to bind. Once baked and cooled, the rectangular slab of pastry, fruit and nuts is inverted and the pastry is anointed with a thick layer of bitter chocolate before cutting into squares.

APRIL

3 MONDAY

4 TUESDAY

5 WEDNESDAY

6 THURSDAY

7 FRIDAY

8 SATURDAY

9 SUNDAY

FLORENTINE PASTRIES

CUTS INTO 24 SQUARES

Kit you'll need:
1 swiss roll tin, 20 x 30cm, greased with butter and base-lined

For The Pâte Sucrée
200g plain flour
¼ teaspoon fine sea salt
100g unsalted butter, chilled
4 medium egg yolks
100g caster sugar
½ teaspoon vanilla extract

For The Topping
90g unsalted butter
50g caster sugar
50g clear honey
175g flaked almonds
50g pistachios, halved
15g chopped candied peel, chopped finer
45g glacé cherries, quartered
3 tablespoons single or whipping cream

To Finish
150g dark chocolate (about 70% cocoa solids), broken up

APRIL

10   MONDAY

11   TUESDAY

Passover (Pesach)
12   WEDNESDAY

13   THURSDAY

14   FRIDAY

Good Friday (UK)
15   SATURDAY

16   SUNDAY

Easter Sunday

FLORENTINE PASTRIES

1 To make the pâte sucrée, sift the flour and salt on to the worktop and make a large well in the centre. Place the butter between 2 sheets of clingfilm and pound with a rolling pin until very supple but still cold. Unwrap the butter and cut it into small pieces, then put it into the well with the egg yolks, sugar and vanilla extract. Gather the fingertips of one of your hands together to form a beak shape and use to mash together the ingredients in the well. When they are thoroughly combined, gradually work in the flour with your fingers, using a plastic dough scraper (or metal spatula) to help you draw the flour in. When the mixture looks like coarse crumbs, gather the whole lot together to make a ball of dough.

2 Lightly dust the worktop with flour, then work the dough gently (pâtissiers call this 'fraiser'): press down on the side of the dough furthest from you with the heel of one hand and push it away from you, then gather up the dough into a ball once more (use the scraper) and repeat. Continue working the dough like this for a couple of minutes – no more – until the dough is silky-smooth and very pliable, so pliable it can be pulled off the worktop in one piece. Form the dough into a thick disc, wrap in clingfilm and chill for 15 minutes.

3. Roll out the pastry dough on the lightly floured worktop to a 20 x 30cm rectangle. Dust the rolling pin with flour, then gently roll the pastry around the pin and lift it into the prepared swiss roll tin. Press it evenly over the base, making sure the corners are filled and there are no gaps between the pastry and the sides of the tin. Prick the pastry base all over with a fork, then cover the tin lightly with clingfilm and chill for 15 minutes.

4 Heat the oven to 180°C/350°F/gas 4. Uncover the pastry and bake for about 15 minutes until lightly golden and firm. Remove the tin from the oven and set it on a heatproof surface. Reduce the oven temperature to 170°C/325°F/gas 3.

5. To make the topping, put the butter, sugar and honey into a large frying pan (preferably non-stick) and heat gently until smoothly melted. Add the almonds, pistachios, peel and cherries and cook over medium/low heat, stirring constantly, for 2–3 minutes until the mixture is a pale straw colour. Stir in the cream and cook for a few more seconds until bubbling, then pour over the pastry base and spread out into an even layer.

6 Bake in the heated oven for about 15 minutes until the topping is a rich golden brown – check after 10 minutes and rotate the tin so the mixture bakes evenly. Transfer the tin to a wire rack. Carefully run a round-bladed knife around the inside of the tin to loosen the sticky mixture, then leave until completely cold.

7 When you're ready to finish the pastries, carefully invert the tin on to a large sheet of baking paper laid on the worktop or a chopping board, then lift off the tin; the underside of the pastry base will now be on top. Put the chocolate into a heatproof bowl and melt gently. Pour the melted chocolate on to the pastry and spread it out evenly in a thick layer using an offset or regular palette knife. Allow to firm up for a few seconds, then use a fork or a plastic pastry comb to mark waves through the chocolate. Leave on the worktop for about 10 minutes until the chocolate is no longer glossy-looking but is matt, set and firm.

8 Turn the Florentine pastry nut-side up on the chopping board. Trim off the edges with a very sharp knife to neaten them, then cut into squares. Press any nuts that fall off back in place. Store in an airtight container at cool room temperature. Best eaten within 4 days.

APRIL

17 — MONDAY

Easter Monday (UK & Republic of Ireland)

18 — TUESDAY

19 — WEDNESDAY

20 — THURSDAY

21 — FRIDAY

22 — SATURDAY

23 — SUNDAY

St. George's Day (England)

NOTES

APRIL

24 MONDAY
ⓟ

25 TUESDAY

26 WEDNESDAY

27 THURSDAY

28 (I lasted 9 weeks) FRIDAY
Environ 3 (2)

29 SATURDAY

30 SUNDAY

NOTES

MAY

1 MONDAY

May Day Holiday (UK & Republic of Ireland)

2 TUESDAY

3 WEDNESDAY

4 THURSDAY

5 FRIDAY

6 SATURDAY

7 SUNDAY

CHOCOLATE & CARAMEL CUSTARD TART

Custard tart meets millionaire's shortbread (a big favourite amongst the Bakers) in this elegant twist on a classic recipe. The crisp pastry case, reminiscent of shortbread, is filled with a rich, creamy, caramel custard and finished with a thick layer of dark chocolate shavings. Don't waste the left-over egg whites – keep them for meringues. If you can't use them straight away they freeze well.

MAY

8 MONDAY

9 TUESDAY

10 WEDNESDAY

11 THURSDAY

12 FRIDAY

13 SATURDAY

14 SUNDAY

CHOCOLATE & CARAMEL CUSTARD TART

SERVES 8-10

Kit you'll need:
1 x 23cm fluted round, deep, loose-based flan tin; a baking sheet

For The Sweet Shortcrust Pastry
175g plain flour
pinch of salt
1 tablespoon caster sugar
100g unsalted butter, chilled and diced
about 2 tablespoons icy cold water
1 medium egg white, for brushing

For The Filling
125g caster sugar, plus 1 tablespoon
125ml water
90g unsalted butter, at room temperature, diced
500ml double cream, at room temperature
7 medium egg yolks, at room temperature
Pinch of fine sea salt

To Finish
50g dark chocolate (about 70% cocoa solids), chopped

MAY

15   MONDAY

16   TUESDAY

17   WEDNESDAY

18   THURSDAY

19   FRIDAY

20   SATURDAY

ⓟ

21   SUNDAY

CHOCOLATE & CARAMEL CUSTARD TART

1 You can make the pastry in a food processor or by hand. For the processor method, put the flour, salt and sugar into the bowl and 'pulse' a couple of times to combine. Add the pieces of butter and blitz until the mixture looks like fine crumbs. Add the cold water and blitz just until the mixture comes together to make a firm dough – if there are dry crumbs and the mixture won't bind together, add more water a teaspoon at a time through the feed tube.

2 To make the pastry by hand, sift the flour, salt and sugar into a mixing bowl. Add the pieces of butter and toss in the flour to lightly coat, then rub the butter into the flour until the mixture looks like fine crumbs. Add the water and stir into the crumbs with a round-bladed knife to make a firm dough; if there are any dry crumbs work in more cold water a teaspoon at time.

3 Shape the dough into a thick disc, wrap it in clingfilm and chill for 20 minutes.

4 Roll out the pastry dough on a lightly floured worktop to a large disc about 32cm across and use to line the flan tin. Leave the excess pastry hanging over the rim for now. Prick the base with a fork and chill the pastry case for 15 minutes.

5 Heat the oven to 190°C/375°F/gas 5. Neaten the edge of the pastry case, trimming off the excess pastry. Line the case with greaseproof paper, fill with baking beans and bake blind in the heated oven for 12-15 minutes until the pastry is set and firm. Remove the paper and beans, then bake the empty case for a further 5-7 minutes until the pastry is crisp and lightly coloured.

6 Transfer the tin to a heatproof surface and quickly brush the inside of the hot pastry case with a thin layer of beaten egg white. This will help to seal the pastry and keep it crisp. Reduce the oven temperature to 170°C/325°F/gas 3, and put the baking sheet into the oven to heat up.

7 Start making the filling while the pastry case is chilling (end of step 4). Put the 125g sugar and the water in a medium pan, set over low heat and stir occasionally to help dissolve the sugar – do not allow the syrup to boil before all the sugar has dissolved. Once the syrup is clear, bring it to the boil and let it boil rapidly until it has turned a rich chestnut brown. Remove from the heat and stir in the pieces of butter, followed by the cream – the mixture will turn lumpy, so return the pan to medium/low heat and stir until melted and smooth. Leave to cool until lukewarm.

8 Put the yolks in a heatproof bowl with the remaining tablespoon of sugar and beat well with a wooden spoon for about 1 minute until very light and smooth. Stir in the lukewarm caramel cream and the salt, then transfer the caramel custard to a large jug.

9 Set the flan tin on the heated baking sheet and place this on the oven shelf. Carefully pour the custard into the pastry case, then gently slide the shelf in and close the oven door. Bake the tart for 25-30 minutes until the custard is just set when you jiggle the baking sheet. Remove from the oven and set the tin on a wire rack. Leave the tart until completely cold.

10 Meanwhile, make chocolate shavings to decorate the tart.

11 Carefully unmould the tart and set it on a serving plate. Transfer the chocolate shavings to the top of the tart using a palette knife rather than your fingers. Serve at room temperature, the same or the next day – keep in an airtight container in the fridge but remove 30 minutes before serving.

MAY

22 — MONDAY

23 — TUESDAY

24 — WEDNESDAY

25 — THURSDAY

26 — FRIDAY

27 — SATURDAY

28 — SUNDAY

NOTES

MAY / JUNE

29 MONDAY

Spring Holiday (UK)
30 TUESDAY

31 WEDNESDAY

1 THURSDAY

2 FRIDAY

3 SATURDAY

4 SUNDAY

FRANGIPANE TART

A really good-looking fruit-topped almond tart to make when succulent peaches and berries are in season, or at any time of the year using tinned or frozen fruit.

JUNE

5 MONDAY

6 TUESDAY

7 WEDNESDAY

8 THURSDAY

9 FRIDAY

10 SATURDAY

11 SUNDAY

FRANGIPANE TART

SERVES 8-10

Kit you'll need:
1 baking sheet; a 28cm fluted round, deep, loose-based flan tin.

For The Pastry
225g plain flour
100g unsalted butter, chilled and diced
50g caster sugar
1 medium egg
1 tablespoon icy cold water

For The Almond Filling
175g unsalted butter, softened
175g caster sugar
4 medium eggs, at room temperature, beaten to mix
175g ground almonds
1 teaspoon almond extract
generous ½ jar home-made raspberry jam OR best-quality shop-bought jam

To Decorate
3 ripe peaches OR 1 x 420g tin sliced peaches
200g raspberries
4 tablespoons apricot jam

JUNE

12   MONDAY

13   TUESDAY

14   WEDNESDAY

15   THURSDAY

16   FRIDAY

17   SATURDAY

18   SUNDAY

Father's Day

FRANGIPANE TART

1 Make the rich sweet shortcrust pastry either by hand or in a food processor. By hand, sift the flour into a bowl, add the diced butter and rub in until the mixture looks like fine crumbs. Stir in the sugar. Beat the egg with the water until combined, then stir into the crumbs with a round-bladed knife to make a slightly soft but not sticky dough. To use a food processor, put the flour and butter into the bowl and blitz until the mixture looks like fine crumbs. Add the sugar and 'pulse' to combine. Mix the egg with the water and, with the machine running, add through the feed tube. Stop the machine as soon as a ball of dough forms. Wrap the dough and chill for 20 minutes until firm but not hard.

2 Heat the oven to 190°C/375°F/gas 5, and put the baking sheet in to heat up. Roll out the pastry on a lightly floured worktop and use to line the flan tin. Prick the base of the pastry case well with a fork, then chill for 10 minutes.

3 Line the pastry case with baking paper and fill with baking beans, then set the tin on the heated baking sheet and bake blind for about 15 minutes until the pastry is set and the edges are lightly coloured. Remove the paper and beans and return the empty pastry case to the oven to bake for a further 10-12 minutes until the base is cooked through (no damp patches) and turning a light golden colour. Set aside to cool (leave the oven on).

4 Now make the almond filling. Put the soft butter and sugar into the food processor (no need to wash the bowl) and blitz until the mixture is creamy and smooth. With the machine running, pour in the eggs through the feed tube. Once combined, stop the machine and scrape down the side of the bowl. Add the ground almonds and almond extract and blitz just until combined. You can also make the filling by hand: cream the butter with the sugar until light and fluffy using a wooden spoon or hand-held electric whisk, then gradually beat in the eggs. Fold in the almonds and almond extract.

5 Spread a thin layer of raspberry jam over the base of the pastry case. Spoon the almond mixture on top and spread evenly. Bake in the heated oven for 30-40 minutes until the filling is golden and feels springy when gently pressed in the centre. Remove the tart from the oven and leave to cool.

6 Once the tart is cold, start on the decoration. If you are using fresh peaches they need to be peeled. To do this, make a small nick in the skin near the stem end, then lower the peaches into a pan of boiling water and leave for 10 seconds. Drain, then peel off the loosened skins with the help of a small sharp knife. Halve the peaches and remove the stones, then cut into thick slices. If using tinned peaches, drain thoroughly.

7 Arrange the peach slices and raspberries in neat circles on top of the tart. Warm the apricot jam in a small pan over low heat, then press through a fine sieve to remove any lumps of fruit. If necessary, reheat the sieved jam so it is nice and runny, then gently brush it over the fruit to glaze. Leave to set before serving.

JUNE

19   MONDAY

20   TUESDAY

21   WEDNESDAY

Longest Day
22   THURSDAY

23   FRIDAY

24   SATURDAY

25   SUNDAY

NOTES

Get new bottle of Environ c/- 23rd June

JUNE / JULY

26 MONDAY

27 TUESDAY

28 WEDNESDAY

29 THURSDAY

30 Envan 3 (3) FRIDAY

1 SATURDAY

2 SUNDAY

PASSIONFRUIT & PINEAPPLE ICE-CREAM ROLL

An impressive dessert for a birthday celebration, made with a decorated lemon sponge and finished with toasted Italian meringue rosettes and chocolate flowers or swirls. This is from the dairy-free ice-cream roll Challenge so coconut milk is used for the custard-based passionfruit ice-cream filling. There is also a fresh pineapple jam to be made, so plenty of work, but worth it!

JULY

3 MONDAY

4 TUESDAY

5 WEDNESDAY

6 THURSDAY

7 FRIDAY

8 SATURDAY

9 SUNDAY

PASSIONFRUIT & PINEAPPLE ICE-CREAM ROLL

SERVES 6-8

Kit you'll need:
A sugar thermometer; an ice-cream maker (optional); a piping bag fitted with a No. 3 fine writing nozzle; a 20 x 30cm swiss roll tin, lined and lightly brushed with oil; a large piping bag fitted with a large star nozzle; a kitchen blowtorch; a small disposable piping bag.

For The Ice Cream
1 x 400g tin coconut milk (not reduced fat)
6 medium egg yolks, at room temperature
130g clear Acacia honey
55g golden syrup
175ml passionfruit juice (sieved from about 15 passionfruit or ready-squeezed juice), chilled

For The Sponge Decoration
1 large egg, at room temperature
30g golden caster sugar
25g plain flour
10g cocoa powder

For The Lemon Sponge
3 large eggs, at room temperature
100g golden caster sugar
½-1 teaspoon lemon extract, to taste
1-3 drops of yellow food colouring
75g self-raising flour

For The Pineapple Jam
450g ready-prepared chopped fresh pineapple
1 small Bramley apple
265g caster sugar
5 tablespoons lemon juice
3 tablespoons bottled apple pectin

For The Italian Meringue
70g egg whites (from 2 large eggs), at room temperature
140g white caster sugar
3 tablespoons water

To Decorate
50g dark chocolate (about 70% cocoa solids), broken up
2 passionfruit

JULY

10   MONDAY

11   TUESDAY

12   WEDNESDAY

Holiday (Northern Ireland)
13 Ⓟ   THURSDAY

14   FRIDAY

15   SATURDAY

16   SUNDAY

PASSIONFRUIT & PINEAPPLE ICE-CREAM ROLL

1 To make the ice cream, put the coconut milk and egg yolks into a medium pan and stir with a wooden spoon over low heat until the mixture reaches 75°C and has slightly thickened to lightly coat the back of the spoon. Remove from the heat and stir in the honey and golden syrup. When the mixture is smooth, stir in the passionfruit juice. Cool quickly by setting the pan in a sink of icy water. Once the mixture is very cold, transfer it to the ice-cream maker and churn until just frozen. Scoop the ice cream into a plastic container and keep in the freezer until needed. (The ice cream can also be made in a container in the freezer; stir the mixture well every 15 minutes until it is evenly firm.)

2 Heat the oven to 180°C/350°F/gas 4. Start by making the sponge decoration. Put the egg and sugar into a bowl and whisk with a hand-held electric whisk until the mixture reaches the ribbon stage. Sift the flour and cocoa powder into the bowl and carefully fold in. Transfer the mixture to the piping bag fitted with the writing nozzle and pipe a diagonal lattice over the base of the lined swiss roll tin. Put it into the freezer to chill while you make the lemon sponge.

3 Break the eggs into a mixing bowl, or the bowl of a free-standing electric mixer, add the sugar and whisk to the ribbon stage. Add lemon extract to taste and the yellow colouring and whisk briefly until evenly combined (without streaks). Sift the flour into the bowl and fold in. Carefully spoon the mixture into the swiss roll tin, on top of the piped lattice, and spread evenly with a palette knife.

4 Bake in the heated oven for about 13 minutes until the sponge is golden and springy when lightly pressed. Set a sheet of baking paper on top of the sponge and then a chopping board (or wire rack). Holding them together, invert the whole thing. Lift off the tin and carefully peel off the lining paper, then cover the sponge with a second sheet of baking paper. Set a wire rack on top and invert so the sponge is now crust-side up. Leave the sheet of baking paper in place, then quickly roll up the hot sponge, from one short side, around a hollow tube or bottle about 7.5cm in diameter. The lattice pattern will be on the outside. Leave to cool.

5 To make the jam, finely chop the pineapple and put into a large pan. Peel, core and finely chop the apple. Add to the pan with the sugar, lemon juice and pectin. Set over medium/low heat and stir gently until the sugar has completely dissolved, then bring to the boil. Boil, stirring frequently, until the jam reaches 104°C on the sugar thermometer or setting point. Pour the jam into a heatproof bowl and leave until completely cold and set. The jam will need to be easy to spread (but not a purée) so, if necessary, blitz it briefly in a food processor.

6 To assemble the roll, carefully unroll the sponge and spread it with a thick layer of jam (you won't need all of it). Working quickly, scoop the ice cream out of the container and on to the middle of the sponge to form a neat log 20 x 7.5cm (you may not need all the ice cream), then roll the sponge around the ice cream. Wrap the roll tightly in clingfilm to hold it all together, then place it in the freezer to firm up.

7 In the meantime, make the meringue. Put the egg whites into a large mixing bowl, or the bowl of a free-standing mixer, and whisk just until frothy. Gently heat the sugar with the water in a small pan, stirring until the sugar has dissolved, then bring to the boil. Boil until the syrup reaches 110°C, then start whisking the whites until they will stand in stiff peaks. As soon as the syrup reaches 118°C, slowly pour it on to the whites while whisking at top speed. Continue whisking until the meringue is stiff and cool.

8 Transfer the meringue to the piping bag fitted with the star nozzle. Unwrap the roll and set it on a freezerproof serving plate. Quickly pipe the meringue along the top of the roll to make 3 rows of 6 rosettes each. Lightly tinge the peaks brown using the kitchen blowtorch. Return the roll to the freezer.

9 For the piped chocolate decorations, melt the chocolate in a heatproof bowl set over a pan of steaming hot water, then temper it: slightly increase the heat under the pan so the temperature of the chocolate rises to 45°C – keep stirring so the chocolate heats evenly. Remove the bowl from the pan and set it in a larger bowl of cold water to quickly cool the chocolate. Gently stir until the temperature falls to 27°C. Set the bowl over the pan of hot water again and reheat the chocolate, stirring, until it reaches 29–30°C. Remove the bowl from the pan and cool slightly. Spoon the chocolate into the small disposable piping bag, snip off the tip and pipe small, neat swirls or flowers on to a sheet of silicone paper – you will need 5 perfect decorations but make extra in case of breakages. Leave until set.

10 To serve, peel the chocolate decorations off the paper and gently press into the meringue. Spoon the passionfruit flesh over the roll and serve immediately.

JULY

17   MONDAY

18   TUESDAY

19   WEDNESDAY

20   THURSDAY

21   FRIDAY

22   SATURDAY

23   SUNDAY

NOTES

9st 12½
28.8% muscle
BMI - 22.k3
Fat = 24.9%

JULY

24 MONDAY

25 TUESDAY

26 WEDNESDAY

27 THURSDAY

28 FRIDAY

29 SATURDAY

30 SUNDAY

NOTES

25/7/16.
9st 11½ | 9st 13.
28.1% Muscle
24.8% Fat
22.1% BMI

JULY / AUGUST

31   **MONDAY**

1   **TUESDAY**

2   **WEDNESDAY**

3   **THURSDAY**

4   **FRIDAY**

5   **SATURDAY**

6   **SUNDAY**

VICTORIA SANDWICH CAKE

The nation's favourite cake, traditionally the ingredients are calculated by weighing the eggs in their shells and using this weight for the butter, sugar and flour.

AUGUST

7   **MONDAY**

Ⓟ

8   Holiday (Scotland & Republic of Ireland)   **TUESDAY**

9   **WEDNESDAY**

10   **THURSDAY**

11   **FRIDAY**

12   **SATURDAY**

13   **SUNDAY**

VICTORIA SANDWICH CAKE

SERVES 12

Kit you'll need:
2x 20.5cm round deep sandwich cake tins

For The Sponge
3 medium eggs, at room temperature
about 175g unsalted butter, softened
about 175g caster sugar
¾ teaspoon vanilla extract
about 175g self-raising flour
1 tablespoon water from the warm water tap

For The Filling
6 tablespoons good-quality raspberry jam
150ml double or whipping cream, well chilled (optional)
Icing sugar, for dusting

AUGUST

14 MONDAY

15 TUESDAY

16 WEDNESDAY

17 THURSDAY

18 FRIDAY

19 SATURDAY

20 SUNDAY

VICTORIA SANDWICH CAKE

1 Preheat the oven to 180°C (160°C fan), 350°F, Gas 4. Grease and line the cake tins with butter and baking paper.

2 Weigh the eggs – 3 medium eggs in their shells weigh around 175g – then use this same weight for the butter, sugar and flour.

3 Put the soft (but not oily) butter into a large mixing bowl or the bowl of a food-mixer and beat well with a wooden spoon or the whisk attachment until very creamy and mayonnaise-like. Scrape down any butter mixture from the sides of the bowl with a plastic spatula, then gradually beat in the sugar a couple of tablespoons at a time. Scrape the mixture off the sides of the bowl again and beat well for 1 minute or until the mixture looks very light and fluffy. Scrape down the mixture again.

4 Break the 3 eggs into a small jug, add the ¾ teaspoon vanilla extract and beat with a fork just until the eggs are broken up. Gradually add to the butter mixture a tablespoon at a time, beating well after each addition and scraping down the sides of the bowl from time to time. If the mixture looks like it might be 'splitting' or curdling, rather than appearing smooth and creamy, stir in a tablespoon of the flour with each of the last two additions of egg.

5 Sift the rest of the flour onto the mixture. Start to gently fold in the flour with a large metal spoon or plastic spatula and after two or three movements add the warm water. Keep folding in until the flour is well mixed in and there are no streaks.

6 Divide the mixture between the two prepared tins – if you want to be really precise, use your scales, or just do it by eye, then spread it evenly.

7 Bake for 20–25 minutes until the sponges are a light golden brown, starting to shrink back from the sides of the tin. Check the sponges after 15 minutes and if they aren't baking evenly, rotate the trays. Check that the sponge springs back when lightly pressed in the middle.

8 When cooked, take them out of the oven and run a round-bladed knife around the outside of each tin to loosen the sponge. Leave for a minute to firm up, then carefully turn out the cakes onto a wire rack. Leave until they are completely cooled.

9 If you are using cream, put a bowl and whisk (or whisk attachment) in the fridge to chill.

10 To assemble the cake, set one sponge crust-side down on a serving plate. Using the back of a tablespoon, evenly spread the sponge with the 6 tablespoons raspberry jam.

11 Pour the cream, if using, into the chilled bowl and whip with the chilled whisk or attachment until it thickens and soft peaks form when you lift out the whisk. Spoon the cream onto the cake and then gently smooth it evenly over the jam. Top with the second sponge, crust-side up, and dust with icing sugar.

AUGUST

21 MONDAY

22 TUESDAY

23 WEDNESDAY

24 THURSDAY

25 FRIDAY

26 SATURDAY

27 SUNDAY

NOTES

Buy Enron 4.

AUGUST / SEPTEMBER

28 MONDAY

Late Summer Holiday (UK)
29 TUESDAY

30 WEDNESDAY

31 THURSDAY

1 FRIDAY

2 SATURDAY

3 SUNDAY

SUGAR-FREE GRAPEFRUIT POLENTA CAKE

British cooks have really embraced all things Italian. Polenta is one ingredient that has been happily adopted, here with ground almonds giving a lovely texture to a cake. Refined sugar is replaced by clear, mild acacia honey and there is more honey in the soaking syrup along with grapefruit and blood orange juices. The unusual topping is made from heavily reduced maple syrup mixed with creamy mascarpone.

SEPTEMBER

4 ⓟ   **MONDAY**

5   **TUESDAY**

6   **WEDNESDAY**

7   **THURSDAY**

Started Emiron ④
8   **FRIDAY**

9   **SATURDAY**

10   **SUNDAY**

SUGAR-FREE GRAPEFRUIT POLENTA CAKE

SERVES 8-10

Kit you'll need:
1 x 20.5cm round, deep cake tin (not loose-based), lined and then brushed with melted butter; a baking sheet; a sugar thermometer.

For The Cake Mixture
150g ground almonds
70g polenta
80g plain flour
1 teaspoon bicarbonate of soda
200g unsalted butter, softened
140g clear Acacia honey
finely grated zest of 1 large red grapefruit
2 large eggs, at room temperature, beaten to mix

For The Citrus Soaking Syrup
200ml freshly squeezed red grapefruit juice
200ml blood orange juice (freshly squeezed if possible)
160g clear Acacia honey

For The Mascarpone Cream Topping
150g maple syrup
300g mascarpone, chilled

For The Candied Peel Decoration
1 red grapefruit
2 oranges
250g clear Acacia honey
125ml water

SEPTEMBER

11 — MONDAY

12 — TUESDAY

13 — WEDNESDAY

14 — THURSDAY

15 — FRIDAY

16 — SATURDAY

17 — SUNDAY

SUGAR-FREE GRAPEFRUIT POLENTA CAKE

1 Heat the oven to 170°C/325°F/gas 3. To make the cake, weigh the ground almonds, polenta and flour into a bowl. Add the bicarbonate of soda and mix thoroughly. Set aside. Put the soft butter into a large mixing bowl, or the bowl of a free-standing electric mixer, and beat with a hand-held electric whisk, or the mixer whisk attachment, until creamy. Add the honey and grated grapefruit zest and beat thoroughly until the mixture is very light. Gradually add the eggs, beating well after each addition. With the whisk on slow speed, gradually mix in the polenta mixture until it is all thoroughly combined.

2 Transfer the mixture to the prepared tin and spread evenly. Set the tin on the baking sheet and bake in the heated oven for about 40 minutes until the cake is a good golden brown and a skewer inserted into the centre comes out clean.

3 While the cake is baking, make the soaking syrup. Pour both fruit juices into a medium pan, add the honey and bring to the boil, stirring. Boil rapidly until the syrup reaches 105°C on a sugar thermometer. Remove from the heat and keep warm.

4 When the cake is done, set the tin on a wire rack, Prick the hot cake all over with a skewer, then spoon the syrup evenly over the surface and let it soak into the sponge – do this gradually until the cake will absorb no more syrup. Leave to soak in and cool for at least 30 minutes.

5 To make the topping, weigh the maple syrup into a small pan and set over medium heat. Bring to the boil, then leave the syrup to bubble away until it reaches 108°C. Leave the thick syrup to cool completely. Put the chilled mascarpone in a bowl and beat well with a wooden spoon until smooth and creamy. Add 60g of the cold, thick syrup and beat well. Cover and keep in the fridge until ready to assemble.

6 To make the candied peel decoration, peel very thin strips of zest (the coloured part of the peel) from the grapefruit and oranges, taking care to leave the white pith on the fruit. Put the peel into a medium pan and cover with boiling water from the kettle. Set over medium heat and simmer for 2 minutes. Drain, then return the peel to the pan and repeat this 'blanching' procedure two more times to remove any bitterness. Drain the peel.

7 Put the honey and water into a small pan and heat gently until liquefied, then bring to the boil and leave to bubble away (it will froth up so take care) until it reaches 115°C. Add the peel to the pan and cook gently for 5–7 minutes until the strips of peel turn translucent. Drain and leave to dry on kitchen paper.

8 To assemble, unmould the cake and set it on a serving plate. Spread and swirl the mascarpone mixture on top, then decorate with the strips of candied peel. Serve immediately. Any leftovers can be kept to enjoy the next day.

SEPTEMBER

18 MONDAY

19 TUESDAY

20 WEDNESDAY

21 THURSDAY

Al Hijra, Rosh Hashanah (Jewish New Year) &
The United Nations International Day of Peace
22 FRIDAY

23 SATURDAY

24 SUNDAY

NOTES

SEPTEMBER / OCTOBER

25 MONDAY

26 TUESDAY

27 WEDNESDAY

28 THURSDAY

29 FRIDAY

30 SATURDAY

Yom Kippur (Day of Atonement)
1 SUNDAY

HALLOWE'EN HATS

Long-standing fans of The Great British Bake Off might remember the chocolate teacake challenge in series 3. These fun, sticky treats have all the same elements as the teacakes – biscuit base, marshmallow and chocolate – but are much simpler to make.

OCTOBER

2 — MONDAY

3 — TUESDAY

4 — WEDNESDAY

5 — THURSDAY

6 — FRIDAY

7 — SATURDAY

8 — SUNDAY

HALLOWE'EN HATS

MAKES 24

Kit you'll need:
A 5cm plain round cutter; 1-2 baking sheets, lined with baking paper; a large disposable piping bag

For The Wholemeal Biscuits
75g stoneground plain wholemeal flour
75g stoneground medium oatmeal
75g plain white flour
75g light brown muscovado sugar
¼ teaspoon bicarbonate of soda
¼ teaspoon ground ginger
¼ teaspoon fine sea salt
75g unsalted butter, chilled and diced
2-3 tablespoons milk, chilled

For The Marshmallow
5g (1 teaspoon) powdered gelatine
4 teaspoons cold water
3 medium egg whites, at room temperature
150g caster sugar
2 tablespoons golden syrup

¼ teaspoon fine sea salt
½ vanilla pod, split open

For The Chocolate Coating
250g dark chocolate (about 70% cocoa solids), broken up

OCTOBER

9 — MONDAY

10 — TUESDAY

11 — WEDNESDAY

12 — THURSDAY

13 — FRIDAY

14 — SATURDAY

15 — SUNDAY

HALLOWE'EN HATS

1 To make the biscuits by hand: sift the wholemeal flour, oatmeal, white flour, sugar, bicarbonate of soda, ginger and salt into a mixing bowl. Add any coarse pieces left in the sieve to the bowl, then add the butter. Rub in with your fingertips until the mixture looks like fine crumbs. Add 2 tablespoons of the milk and, using a round-bladed knife, mix to a firm dough, adding more milk as needed to bring the dough together – it should feel like shortcrust pastry.

2 To make the dough in a food processor, put all the ingredients except for the butter and milk in the processor bowl and 'pulse' a few times just to combine everything. Add the pieces of butter and blitz just until the mixture looks like fine crumbs. With the machine running slowly, add enough of the milk through the feed tube to bring the mixture together into a ball of fairly firm dough. Flatten the dough to a thick disc, then wrap in clingfilm and chill for 30 minutes.

3 Heat the oven to 190°C/375°F/gas 5. Unwrap the dough and place it between 2 large sheets of clingfilm. Roll out to about 5mm thickness. Peel off the top sheet of clingfilm and stamp out discs with the round cutter. Transfer the discs to the baking sheet, setting them slightly apart to allow for expansion. Gather up the dough trimmings and gently knead them together, then re-roll as before and cut more discs. Prick the discs all over with a fork.

4 Bake in the heated oven for 13–15 minutes until golden with slightly darker edges – check after 10 minutes and rotate the baking sheets, if necessary, so the biscuits bake evenly. Remove from the oven and leave the biscuits on the baking sheet for a minute to firm up slightly, then transfer to a wire rack to cool. (The biscuits can be made up to 4 days in advance and stored in an airtight container.)

5 To make the marshmallow, sprinkle the gelatine over the cold water in a small heatproof bowl or cup. Leave to 'sponge' for 5 minutes, then set the bowl in a larger bowl or pan of very hot but not boiling water and leave the gelatine to dissolve.

6 Meanwhile, put the egg whites, caster sugar, golden syrup and salt in a large heatproof mixing bowl. Scrape the seeds from the vanilla pod (discard the pod) and add to the bowl. Set over a pan of simmering water (the base of the bowl shouldn't touch the water) and whisk with a hand-held electric whisk on full speed for 1 minute. Whisk in the gelatine mixture, then continue whisking for about 8 minutes until you have a glossy, silky-smooth and very stiff meringue-like mixture.

7 Remove the bowl from the pan and whisk for another 8 minutes until the mixture has cooled. Spoon the marshmallow mixture into the piping bag.

8 Arrange the biscuits, slightly apart, on a wire rack. Snip the end off the piping bag to make a 1.5cm opening. Holding the bag vertically above each biscuit, pipe a cone of marshmallow on top, about 5cm high and 4cm wide at its base; pull the bag up sharply to leave a peak that looks like a witch's pointy hat. There's enough marshmallow mixture to allow for some mistakes, so if the peaked cones lean to one side or you just don't like the way they look, scrape them off and start again. Leave the biscuits, uncovered, on the worktop for about 2 hours until the marshmallow has set.

9 When ready to finish, melt the chocolate, then leave to cool for a minute. Place a baking sheet under the wire rack (to catch the drips) before carefully spooning the chocolate over the witches' hats to completely cover the marshmallow and the biscuit rim. Once you have coated all the hats, scoop up the drips underneath the rack and use to touch up any bare spots. Leave until set. Best eaten the same or the next day – store in an airtight container in a cool spot (not in the fridge).

Tip: You can make larger wholemeal biscuits to enjoy with coffee. Stamp out with a 7cm cutter and bake for 14–15 minutes.

OCTOBER

16   MONDAY

17   TUESDAY

18   WEDNESDAY

19   THURSDAY

Diwali
20   FRIDAY

21   SATURDAY

22   SUNDAY

NOTES

# OCTOBER

23 .... MONDAY

24 .... TUESDAY

25 .... WEDNESDAY

26 ⓟ .... THURSDAY

27 .... FRIDAY

28 .... SATURDAY

29 .... SUNDAY

Daylight Saving Ends

NOTES

Buy Environ ④

OCTOBER / NOVEMBER

30 MONDAY

31 TUESDAY
Holiday (Republic of Ireland)

1 WEDNESDAY
Halloween

2 THURSDAY

3 FRIDAY

4 SATURDAY

5 SUNDAY
Guy Fawkes Night

BONFIRE CHILLI WITH CORNBREAD TOPPING

On Bonfire Night, you need good hot food so a home-made chilli is spot on, here with a tasty, fluffy Texas-style cornbread topping, dropped on top of the bubbling chilli like dumplings, towards the end of its time in the oven. If you want some fire in your cornbread as well, you can use chopped green chilli instead of chives. A bowl of soured cream and a good green salad complete the meal.

NOVEMBER

6 — MONDAY

7 — TUESDAY

8 — WEDNESDAY

9 — THURSDAY

10 — FRIDAY

11 — SATURDAY

12 — SUNDAY

Remembrance Sunday

BONFIRE CHILLI WITH CORNBREAD TOPPING

SERVES 4-6

Kit you'll need:
A large flameproof casserole with lid (see recipe).

For The Chilli
2 tablespoons rapeseed oil
450g lean minced beef
1 large red onion, finely chopped
4 garlic cloves, or to taste, crushed
½–1 teaspoon hot/mild chilli powder, to taste
1 teaspoon ground cumin
1 tablespoon tomato purée
2 x 400g tins chopped tomatoes
3 tablespoons water
2 medium red peppers, cored and cut into 2cm chunks
1 x 400g tin red kidney beans, drained and rinsed
salt and pepper, to taste

For The Cornbread Topping
140g medium/fine yellow cornmeal OR polenta
125g plain flour
½ teaspoon bicarbonate of soda
1 teaspoon baking powder
¼ teaspoon fine sea salt
small bunch of fresh chives, finely snipped
225ml buttermilk
1 medium egg
1 tablespoon clear honey
50g unsalted butter, melted

To Serve
soured cream

NOVEMBER

13 — MONDAY

14 — TUESDAY

15 — WEDNESDAY

16 — THURSDAY

17 — FRIDAY

18 — SATURDAY

19 — SUNDAY

BONFIRE CHILLI WITH CORNBREAD TOPPING

1 Heat the oven to 180°C/350°F/gas 4. Heat the oil in the casserole over medium/high heat. (If your casserole isn't flameproof, you can cook the chilli on top of the stove in a large saucepan, then transfer it to a casserole before adding the topping.) Add the beef and fry, stirring constantly, until lightly coloured and broken up. Push the meat to one side and turn down the heat, then add the chopped onion to the other side of the casserole. Cook gently, stirring occasionally, for about 7 minutes until softened but not browned. Add the garlic, ½ teaspoon chilli powder, the cumin, a good pinch each of salt and pepper and the tomato purée. Stir everything together. Cook for a further 2 minutes, stirring frequently.

2 Add the tomatoes to the casserole. Pour the water into one empty tomato tin and swish it around to clean it out, then tip the water into the second tin, swish it around and pour into the casserole. Stir well and bring the mixture to the boil. Cover with the lid and transfer the casserole to the oven. Cook for 30 minutes. (If you are simmering the chilli in a covered pan on top of the stove, stir occasionally.)

3 Stir the chilli well, then stir in the red peppers and beans. Cover again and return to the oven to cook for 15 minutes.

4 Remove the chilli from the oven (leave the oven on) and give it a stir. Taste and add more chilli powder, salt and pepper as needed, so it has just the right amount of 'heat' for your family or guests. If you have made the chilli in a saucepan, transfer it to a casserole. Set aside.

5 To make the topping, combine the cornmeal, flour, bicarbonate of soda, baking powder, salt, chives and 3-4 grinds of pepper in a mixing bowl and make a well in the centre. Measure the buttermilk in a jug and add the egg, honey and melted butter. Mix with a fork, then pour into the well. Stir everything together thoroughly using a wooden spoon – the mixture will be thick and sticky.

6 Drop heaped spoonfuls of the cornbread mixture on top of the chilli to cover the surface. Leave the cornbread mounds looking rough – don't spread them out – so there is a little space between them for the sauce to bubble up. Place in the heated oven and bake for about 30 minutes until the chilli is bubbling and the cornbread topping is set and a nice golden brown. Serve piping hot, with soured cream.

Tip: The chilli can be made ahead, then left to cool and kept, tightly covered, in the fridge for up to 3 days. Bring the chilli back to the boil on top of the stove before adding the topping. If the chilli seems dry and lacking in sauce, add a little water to loosen it up. If you have any topping left over, form it into golfball-sized mounds and set, slightly apart, on a baking sheet lined with baking paper. Bake alongside the chilli for 20-25 minutes until golden brown.

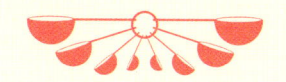

NOVEMBER

20 MONDAY

21 TUESDAY

ⓟ

22 WEDNESDAY

23 THURSDAY

24 FRIDAY

25 SATURDAY

26 Started Emma 4 (2)   SUNDAY

NOTES

NOVEMBER / DECEMBER

27 MONDAY

28 TUESDAY

29 WEDNESDAY

30 THURSDAY

St. Andrew's Day (Scotland)

1 FRIDAY

2 SATURDAY

3 SUNDAY

CHOCOLATE STARS

The chocolate-hazelnut paste popularised by the chocolate-makers of Turin in the 19th century was the forerunner of Nutella, the spread that children all over the world know and love. The dark chocolate-hazelnut ganache that fills these rich chocolate shortbread biscuits is an adult version of that childhood treat. Make these for a special tea party – they can be baked and assembled a day or so in advance.

DECEMBER

4   MONDAY

5   TUESDAY

6   WEDNESDAY

7   THURSDAY

8   FRIDAY

9   SATURDAY

10   SUNDAY

CHOCOLATE STARS

MAKES 20 PAIRS

Kit you'll need:

A 6–7cm star cutter; 2 baking sheets, lined with baking paper; a small disposable piping bag

For The Dough

225g unsalted butter, softened
100g caster sugar
225g plain flour
65g cocoa powder
¼ teaspoon fine sea salt

For The Ganache Filling

75g blanched hazelnuts
1 tablespoon caster sugar
75g dark chocolate (about 70% cocoa solids)
75ml double cream
25g unsalted butter
pinch of salt

To Finish

50g dark chocolate (about 70% cocoa solids)
Icing sugar, for dusting

DECEMBER

11 — MONDAY

12 — TUESDAY

13 — WEDNESDAY

14 — THURSDAY

15 — FRIDAY

16 — SATURDAY

17 — SUNDAY

CHOCOLATE STARS
▼▼▼▼▼▼▼▼▼▼

1 Make the dough first. Put the softened butter into a mixing bowl, or the bowl of a free-standing electric mixer. Beat with a wooden spoon or a hand-held electric whisk, or the whisk attachment of the mixer, until very creamy. Add the sugar and beat until the mixture is much lighter in colour and texture. Scrape down the side of the bowl.

2 Sift the flour, cocoa powder and salt into the bowl and mix in with a wooden spoon or plastic spatula, then use your hands to bring the mixture together into a firm dough.

3 Turn the dough out on to an unfloured worktop (flour will leave white marks on the dough) and gently knead to a flat disc. (In very warm weather, or if your dough feels soft, wrap it in clingfilm and chill for about 15 minutes until firm enough to roll out.) Place the disc between 2 large sheets of clingfilm and roll out to 5mm thickness. Peel off the top layer of clingfilm and stamp out stars with the cutter. Gather up the trimmings, then re-roll and stamp out more stars. You want an even number – the dough should make 40 stars – but a few extra will allow for breakages.

4 Set the stars, slightly apart to allow for expansion, on the baking sheets, then cover lightly with clingfilm and chill for 15 minutes. Meanwhile, heat your oven to 180°C/350°F/gas 4.

5 Uncover the stars and bake in the heated oven for about 12 minutes until just firm but not coloured – watch them carefully as the chocolate dough can quickly turn very dark around the tips (this would make the biscuits taste bitter). Remove from the oven and leave the stars to firm up on the baking sheets for 3 minutes before carefully transferring them to a wire rack to cool – the biscuits will be very fragile until completely cold. Leave the oven on.

6 While the biscuits are cooling, make the ganache filling. Tip the hazelnuts into a small baking dish or tin and toast in the oven for 7–10 minutes until a good golden brown. Remove 20 of the best-looking nuts and set aside for the decoration. Transfer the rest of the nuts to a food processor (there's no need to wait until they are cold). Add the sugar and process until ground to a fairly fine and slightly sticky powder.

7 Break or chop up the chocolate into even-sized pieces and put into a small, heavy-based pan with the cream, butter and salt. Set over very low heat and stir gently with a wooden spoon until melted and smooth. Remove from the heat and stir in the ground hazelnuts. Leave the ganache on the worktop, stirring frequently, until firm enough to spread.

8 When you are ready to assemble the stars, give the ganache a good stir. Using about a rounded teaspoon of ganache for each, gently spread the ganache over the underside of 20 stars. The biscuits are quite fragile – a tip might break off, but you can 'glue' it back with a dab of ganache. Top each star with a second star, placing the biscuits underside to underside and matching up the points.

9 To finish the stars, gently melt the chocolate. One at a time, dip the rounded base of each whole hazelnut in the melted chocolate, then set it in the centre of a star biscuit. Spoon the rest of the melted chocolate into the piping bag and snip off the end to make a small opening. Quickly pipe a fine zigzag of chocolate across each star. Leave until set, then very lightly dust with icing sugar. Store in an airtight container and eat within 5 days.

DECEMBER

18   MONDAY

ⓟ

19   TUESDAY

20   WEDNESDAY

21   THURSDAY

Shortest Day

22   FRIDAY

23   SATURDAY

24   SUNDAY

NOTES

DECEMBER

25   **MONDAY**

Christmas Day

26   **TUESDAY**

Boxing Day & St. Stephen's Day (Republic of Ireland)

27   **WEDNESDAY**

28   **THURSDAY**

29   **FRIDAY**

30   **SATURDAY**

31   **SUNDAY**

New Year's Eve

NOTES

NOTES

NOTES

NOTES

NOTES

NOTES

NOTES

NOTES

NOTES